MW01143702

A Visit to the Farmers' Market

by Peggy Sissel-Phelan, Ed.D.

Books that are Building Blocks of Healthy Beginnings

A Division of Brain Child Press
www.brainchildpress.com

Published by
Brain Child Books
13324 Beckenham Dr. Suite 100
Little Rock, AR 72212

Design and layout
Peggy Sissel-Phelan

International Standard Book Number (ISBN)
Paper: 978-0-9771010-0-9

5th printing
Printed in the United States of America

Photocredits –   pp. 6, 7, & 8: F. William King and Linda J. King
p. 15: Bill Tarpenning, USDA
All other photos are property of the author.

Brain Child Books is a division of Brain Child Press.
Visit us at www.brainchildpress.com

The Farmers' Market is today.

At the Farmers' Market

there's lots to see

and taste!

The food we buy at
the Farmers' Market

grows on the farm.

It's fresh from the garden.

Fresh foods are best for you.

Eat lots of different kinds,

and the more colorful, the better!

Like red tomatoes,

yellow squash,

and green beans.

Don't forget the fruit!
You might find watermelons,

fresh peaches,

juicy blueberries,

crisp apples,

and fresh pears and plums.

In the fall, you can buy pumpkins!

The Farmers' Market -

where there are new folks to meet

and good things to eat!